The Poetry of William H. D

William Henry Davies was born in the Pillgwenlly district of Newport, Monmouthshire, Wales, a busy port on July 3rd, 1871.

Davies seemed to find childhood difficult. By the age of 13 he was arrested, part of a gang of five schoolmates, and charged with stealing handbags. He was given twelve strokes of the birch. The following year, 1885, Davies wrote his first poem; "Death".

His yearning was to travel. In a half dozen years, he crossed the Atlantic at least annually by working on cattle ships. He travelled through many of the states, sometimes begging, sometimes taking seasonal work, but would often spend any savings on a drinking spree with a fellow traveller.

In London, he came across a newspaper story about the riches to be made in the Klondike and immediately set off to make his fortune in Canada. Attempting to jump a freight train at Renfrew, Ontario, on March 20th, 1899, he lost his footing and his right foot was crushed under the wheels of the train. The leg later had to be amputated below the knee and he wore a wooden prosthetic leg thereafter.

On October 12th, 1905 Davies met the poet Edward Thomas, then the literary critic for the Daily Chronicle. Thomas rented for Davies a nearby tiny two-roomed cottage. Thomas now adopted the role of protective guardian as he helped Davies to develop his career.

In 1907, the manuscript of The Autobiography of a Super-Tramp drew the attention of George Bernard Shaw, who agreed to write a preface.

In 1911, Davies was awarded a Civil List Pension of £50, which later increased to £100 and then to £150.

The Georgian poetry publisher Edward Marsh introduced him, in 1913, to DH Lawrence who was captivated by Davies and later invited him to Germany. Despite this early enthusiasm, Lawrence's opinion waned and he noted the newer verses seemed "so thin, one can hardly feel them".

On February 5th, 1923, Davies married 23-year-old Helen Matilda Payne, at the Registry Office in East Grinstead in Sussex. His book Young Emma chronicles the relationship in a very frank and revealing way. Having second thoughts he retrieved the book from the publishers and it was only published after Helens death. He had met her near Marble Arch decanting from a bus wearing a "saucy-looking little velvet cap with tassels". At the time Helen was unmarried and pregnant. While living with Davies in London, before their marriage, Helen suffered an almost fatal miscarriage.

Davies made over a dozen broadcasts for the BBC, reading his own work, between 1924 and 1940.

Davies returned to Newport, in September 1938, for the unveiling of a plaque in his honour, and with an address given by the Poet Laureate John Masefield. His health had now deteriorated, and this proved to be his last public appearance.

W. H. Davies' health continued to worsen and he died, on September 26th, 1940, at the age of 69.

Index of Contents

THE WORM'S CONTEMPT

What do we earn for all our gentle grace?
A body stiff and cold from foot to face.

If you have beauty, what is beauty worth?
A mask to hide it, made of common earth.

What do we get for all our song and prattle?
A gasp for longer breath, and then a rattle.

What do we earn for dreams, and our high teaching?
The worms' contempt, that have no time for preaching.

THE HAWK

Thou dost not fly, thou art not perched,
The air is all around:
What is it that can keep thee set,
From falling to the ground?
The concentration of thy mind
Supports thee in the air;
As thou dost watch the small young birgs,
With such a deadly care.

My mind has such a hawk as thou,
It is an evil mood;
It comes when there's no cause for grief,
And on my joys doth brood.
Then do I see my life in parts;
The earth receives my bones,
The common air absorbs my mind—
It knows not flowers from stones.

THE HEAP OF RAGS

One night when I went down
Thames' side, in London Town,
A heap of rags saw I,
And sat me down close by.
That thing could shout and bawl,
But showed no face at all;
When any steamer passed
And blew a loud shrill blast,
That heap of rags would sit
And make a sound like it;

When struck the clock's deep bell,
It made those peals as well.
When winds did moan around,
It mocked them with that sound;
When all was quiet, it
Fell into a strange fit;
Would sigh, and moan, and roar,
It laughed, and blessed, and swore.
Yet that poor thing, I know,
Had neither friend nor foe;
Its blessin' or its curse
Made no one better or worse.
I left it in that place—
The thing that showed no face,
Was it a man that had
Suffered till he went mad?
So many showers and not
One rainbow in the lot?
Too many bitter fears
To make a pearl from tears?

THE CHILD AND THE MARINER

A dear old couple my grandparents were,
And kind to all dumb things; they saw in Heaven
The lamb that Jesus petted when a child;
Their faith was never draped by Doubt: to them
Death was a rainbow in Eternity,
That promised everlasting brightness soon.
An old seafaring man was he; a rough
Old man, but kind; and hairy, like the nut
Full of sweet milk. All day on shore he watched
The winds for sailors' wives, and told what ships
Enjoyed fair weather, and what ships had storms;
He watched the sky, and he could tell for sure
What afternoons would follow stormy morns,
If quiet nights would end wild afternoons.
He leapt away from scandal with a roar,
And if a whisper still possessed his mind,
He walked about and cursed it for a plague.
He took offence at Heaven when beggars passed,
And sternly called them back to give them help.
In this old captain's house I lived, and things
That house contained were in ships' cabins once:
Sea-shells and charts and pebbles, model ships;
Green weeds, dried fishes stuffed, and coral stalks;

Old wooden trunks with handles of spliced rope,
With copper saucers full of monies strange,
That seemed the savings of dead men, not touched
To keep them warm since their real owners died;
Strings of red beads, methought were dipped in blood,
And swinging lamps, as though the house might move;
An ivory lighthouse built on ivory rocks,
The bones of fishes and three bottled ships.
And many a thing was there which sailors make
In idle hours, when on long voyages,
Of marvellous patience, to no lovely end.
And on those charts I saw the small black dots
That were called islands, and I knew they had
Turtles and palms, and pirates' buried gold.
There came a stranger to my granddad's house,
The old man's nephew, a seafarer too;
A big, strong able man who could have walked
Twm Barlum's hill all clad in iron mail
So strong he could have made one man his club
To knock down others—Henry was his name,
No other name was uttered by his kin.
And here he was, sooth illclad, but oh,
Thought I, what secrets of the sea are his!
This man knows coral islands in the sea,
And dusky girls heartbroken for white men;
More rich than Spain, when the Phoenicians shipped
Silver for common ballast, and they saw
Horses at silver mangers eating grain;
This man has seen the wind blow up a mermaid's hair
Which, like a golden serpent, reared and stretched
To feel the air away beyond her head.
He begged my pennies, which I gave with joy—
He will most certainly return some time
A self-made king of some new land, and rich.
Alas that he, the hero of my dreams,
Should be his people's scorn; for they had rose
To proud command of ships, whilst he had toiled
Before the mast for years, and well content;
Him they despised, and only Death could bring
A likeness in his face to show like them.
For he drank all his pay, nor went to sea
As long as ale was easy got on shore.
Now, in his last long voyage he had sailed
From Plymouth Sound to where sweet odours fan
The Cingalese at work, and then back home—
But came not near my kin till pay was spent.
He was not old, yet seemed so; for his face
Looked like the drowned man's in the morgue, when it

Has struck the wooden wharves and keels of ships.
And all his flesh was pricked with Indian ink,
His body marked as rare and delicate
As dead men struck by lightning under trees
And pictured with fine twigs and curlèd ferns;
Chains on his neck and anchors on his arms;
Rings on his fingers, bracelets on his wrist;
And on his breast the Jane of Appledore
Was schooner rigged, and in full sail at sea.
He could not whisper with his strong hoarse voice,
No more than could a horse creep quietly;
He laughed to scorn the men that muffled close
For fear of wind, till all their neck was hid,
Like Indian corn wrapped up in long green leaves;
He knew no flowers but seaweeds brown and green,
He knew no birds but those that followed ships.
Full well he knew the water-world; he heard
A grander music there than we on land,
When organ shakes a church; swore he would make
The sea his home, though it was always roused
By such wild storms as never leave Cape Horn;
Happy to hear the tempest grunt and squeal
Like pigs heard dying in a slaughterhouse.
A true-born mariner, and this his hope—
His coffin would be what his cradle was,
A boat to drown in and be sunk at sea;
Salted and iced in Neptune's larder deep.
This man despised small coasters, fishing-smacks;
He scorned those sailors who at night and morn
Can see the coast, when in their little boats
They go a six days' voyage and are back
Home with their wives for every Sabbath day.
Much did he talk of tankards of old beer,
And bottled stuff he drank in other lands,
Which was a liquid fire like Hell to gulp,
But Paradise to sip.

And so he talked;
Nor did those people listen with more awe
To Lazurus—whom they had seen stone dead—
Than did we urchins to that seaman's voice.
He many a tale of wonder told: of where,
At Argostoli, Cephalonia's sea
Ran over the earth's lip in heavy floods;
And then again of how the strange Chinese
Conversed much as our homely Blackbirds sing.
He told us how he sailed in one old ship
Near that volcano Martinique, whose power

Shook like dry leaves the whole Caribbean seas;
And made the sun set in a sea of fire
Which only half was his; and dust was thick
On deck, and stones were pelted at the mast.
Into my greedy ears such words that sleep
Stood at my pillow half the night perplexed.
He told how isles sprang up and sank again,
Between short voyages, to his amaze;
How they did come and go, and cheated charts;
Told how a crew was cursed when one man killed
A bird that perched upon a moving barque;
And how the sea's sharp needles, firm and strong,
Ripped open the bellies of big, iron ships;
Of mighty icebergs in the Northern seas,
That haunt the far horizon like white ghosts.
He told of waves that lift a ship so high
That birds could pass from starboard unto port
Under her dripping keel.

Oh, it was sweet
To hear that seaman tell such wondrous tales:
How deep the sea in parts, that drownèd men
Must go a long way to their graves and sink
Day after day, and wander with the tides.
He spake of his own deeds; of how he sailed
One summer's night along the Bosphorus,
And he—who knew no music like the wash
Of waves against a ship, or wind in shrouds—
Heard then the music on that woody shore
Of nightingales, and feared to leave the deck,
He thought 'twas sailing into Paradise.
To hear these stories all we urchins placed
Our pennies in that seaman's ready hand;
Until one morn he signed on for a long cruise,
And sailed away—we never saw him more.
Could such a man sink in the sea unknown?
Nay, he had found a land with something rich,
That kept his eyes turned inland for his life.
'A damn bad sailor and a landshark too,
No good in port or out'—my granddad said.

THE SLUGGARD

A jar of cider and my pipe,
In summer, under shady tree;
A book by one that made his mind

Live by its sweet simplicity:
Then must I laugh at kings who sit
In richest chambers, signing scrolls;
And princes cheered in public ways,
And stared at by a thousand fools.

Let me be free to wear my dreams,
Like weeds in some mad maiden's hair,
When she believes the earth has not
Another maid so rich and fair;
And proudly smiles on rich and poor,
The queen of all fair women then:
So I, dressen in my idle dreams,
Will think myself the king of men.

THE BOY

Go, little boy,
Fill thee with joy;
For Time gives thee
Unlicensed hours,
To run in fields,
And roll in flowers.

A little boy
Can life enjoy;
If but to see
The horses pass,
When shut indoors
Behind the glass.

Go, little boy,
Fill thee with joy;
Fear not, like man,
The kick of wrath,
That you do lie
In some one's path.

Time is to thee
Eternity,
As to a bird
Or butterfly;
And in that faith
True joy doth lie.

THE HERMIT

What moves that lonely man is not the boom
Of waves that break agains the cliff so strong;
Nor roar of thunder, when that travelling voice
Is caught by rocks that carry far along.

'Tis not the groan of oak tree i its prime,
When lightning strikes its solid heart to dust;
Nor frozen pond when, melted by the sun,
It suddenly doth break its sparkling crust.

What moves that man is when the blind bat taps
His window when he sits alone at night;
Or when the small bird sounds like some great beast
Among the dead, dry leaves so frail and light.

Or when the moths on his night-pillow beat
Such heavy blows he fears they'll break his bones;
Or when a mouse inside the papered walls,
Comes like a tiger crunching through the stones.

THE FLOOD

I thought my true love slept;
Behind her chair I crept
And pulled out a long pin;
The golden flood came out,
She shook it all about,
With both our faces in.

Ah! little wren, I know
Your mossy, small nest now
A windy, cold place is;
No eye can see my face,
Howe'er it watch the place
Where I half drown in bliss.

When I am drowned hald dead,
She laughs and shakes her head;
Flogged by her hair-waves, I
Withdraw my face from there;
But never once, I swear,
She heard a mercy cry.

THE BIRD OF PARADISE

Here comes Kate Summers, who, for gold,
Takes any man to bed:
"You knew my friend, Nell Barnes," she said;
"You knew Nell Barnes—she's dead.

"Nell Barnes was bad on all you men,
Unclean, a thief as well;
Yet all my life I have not found
A better friend than Nell.

"So I sat at her side at last,
For hours, till she was dead;
And yet she had no sense at all
Of any word I said.

"For all her cry but came to this—
'Not for the world! Take care:
Don't touch that bird of paradise,
Perched on the bed-post there!'

"I asked her would she like some grapes,
Some damsons ripe and sweet;
A custard made with new-laid eggs,
Or tender fowl to eat.

"I promised I would follow her,
To see her in her grave;
And buy a wreath with borrowed pence,
If nothing I could save.

"Yet still her cry but came to this—
'Not for the world! Take care:
Don't touch that bird of paradise,
Perched on the bed-post there!' "

THE LIKENESS

When I came forth this morn I saw
Quite twenty cloudlets in the air;
And then I saw a flock of sheep,
Which told me how these clouds came there.

That flock of sheep, on that green grass,
Well might it lie so still and proud!
Its likeness had been drawn in heaven,
On a blue sky, in silvery cloud.

I gazed me up, I gazed me down,
And swore, though good the likeness was,
'Twas a long way from justice done
To such white wool, such sparkling grass.

THE SLEEPERS

As I walked down the waterside
This silent morning, wet and dark;
Before the cocks in farmyards crowed,
Before the dogs began to bark;
Before the hour of five was struck
By old Westminster's mighty clock:

As I walked down the waterside
This morning, in the cold damp air,
I saw a hundred women and men
Huddled in rags and sleeping there:
These people have no work, thought I,
And long before their time they die.

That moment, on the waterside,
A lighted car came at a bound;
I looked inside, and saw a score
Of pale and weary men that frowned;
Each man sat in a huddled heap,
Carried to work while fast asleep.

Ten cars rushed down the waterside
Like lighted coffins in the dark;
With twenty dead men in each car,
That must be brought alive by work:
These people work too hard, thought I,
And long before their time they die.

WHERE WE DIFFER

To think my thoughts are hers,
Not one of hers is mine;

She laughs—while I must sigh;
She sighs—while I must whine.

She eats—while I must fast;
She reads—while I am blind;
She sleeps—while I must wake;
Free—I no freedom find.

To think the world for me
Contains but her alone,
And that her eyes prefer
Some ribbon, scarf, or stone.

THIS NIGHT

This night, as I sit here alone,
And brood on what is dead and gone,
The owl that's in this Highgate Wood,
Has found his fellow in my mood;
To every star, as it doth rise -
Oh-o-o! Oh-o-o! he shivering cries.

And, looking at the Moon this night,
There's that dark shadow in her light.
Ah! Life and death, my fairest one,
Thy lover is a skeleton!
"And why is that?" I question - "why?"
Oh-o-o! Oh-o-o! the owl doth cry.

TRULY GREAT

My walls outside must have some flowers,
My walls within must have some books;
A house that's small; a garden large,
And in it leafy nooks.

A little gold that's sure each week;
That comes not from my living kind,
But from a dead man in his grave,
Who cannot change his mind.

A lovely wife, and gentle too;
Contented that no eyes but mine
Can see her many charms, nor voice

To call her beauty fine.

Where she would in that stone cage live,
A self-made prisoner, with me;
While many a wild bird sang around,
On gate, on bush, on tree.

And she sometimes to answer them,
In her far sweeter voice than all;
Till birds, that loved to look on leaves,
Will doat on a stone wall.

With this small house, this garden large,
This little gold, this lovely mate,
With health in body, peace in heart--
Show me a man more great.

THE MIND'S LIBERTY

The mind, with its own eyes and ears,
May for these others have no care;
No matter where this body is,
The mind is free to go elsewhere.
My mind can be a sailor, when
This body's still confined to land;
And turn these mortals into trees,
That walk in Fleet Street or the Strand.

So, when I'm passing Charing Cross,
Where porters work both night and day,
I ofttimes hear sweet Malpas Brook,
That flows thrice fifty miles away.
And when I'm passing near St Paul's
I see beyond the dome and crowd,
Twm Barlum, that green pap in Gwent,
With its dark nipple in a cloud.

WHEN ON A SUMMER'S MORN

When on a summer's morn I wake,
And open my two eyes,
Out to the clear, born-singing rills
My bird-like spirit flies.

To hear the Blackbird, Cuckoo, Thrush,
Or any bird in song;
And common leaves that hum all day
Without a throat or tongue.

And when Time strikes the hour for sleep,
Back in my room alone,
My heart has many a sweet bird's song --
And one that's all my own.

THE DARK HOUR

And now, when merry winds do blow,
And rain makes trees look fresh,
An overpowering staleness holds
This mortal flesh.

Though well I love to feel the rain,
And be by winds well blown—
The mystery of mortal life
Doth press me down.

And, In this mood, come now what will,
Shine Rainbow, Cuckoo call;
There is no thing in Heaven or Earth
Can lift my soul.

I know not where this state comes from—
No cause for grief I know;
The Earth around is fresh and green,
Flowers near me grow.

I sit between two fair rose trees;
Red roses on my right,
And on my left side roses are
A lovely white.

The little birds are full of joy,
Lambs bleating all the day;
The colt runs after the old mare,
And children play.

And still there comes this dark, dark hour—
Which is not borne of Care;
Into my heart it creeps before
I am aware.

SEEKING BEAUTY

Cold winds can never freeze, nor thunder sour
The cup of cheer that Beauty draws for me
Out of those Azure heavens and this green earth—
I drink and drink, and thirst the more I see.

To see the dewdrops thrill the blades of grass,
Makes my whole body shake; for here's my choice
Of either sun or shade, and both are green—
A Chaffinch laughs in his melodious voice.

The banks are stormed by Speedwell, that blue flower
So like a little heaven with one star out;
I see an amber lake of buttercups,
And Hawthorn foams the hedges round about.

The old Oak tree looks now so green and young,
That even swallows perch awhile and sing:
This is that time of year, so sweet and warm,
When bats wait not for stars ere they take wing.

As long as I love Beauty I am young,
Am young or old as I love more or less;
When Beauty is not heeded or seems stale,
My life's a cheat, let Death end my distress.

THE HAPPY CHILD

I saw this day sweet flowers grow thick—
But not one like the child did pick.

I heard the pack-hounds in green park—
But no dog like the child heard bark.

I heard this day bird after bird—
But not one like the child has heard.

A hundred butterflies saw I—
But not one like the child saw fly.

I saw the horses roll in grass—
But no horse like the child saw pass.

My world this day has lovely been—
But not like what the child has seen.

SONGS OF JOY

Sing out, my soul, thy songs of joy;
Sing as a happy bird will sing
Beneath a rainbow's lovely arch
In the spring.

Think not of death in thy young days;
Why shouldst thou that grim tyrant fear?
And fear him not when thou art old,
And he is near.

Strive not for gold, for greedy fools
Measure themselves by poor men never;
Their standard still being richer men,
Makes them poor ever.

Train up thy mind to feel content,
What matters then how low thy store?
What we enjoy, and not possess,
Makes rich or poor.

Filled with sweet thought, then happy I
Take not my state from other's eyes;
What's in my mind—not on my flesh
Or theirs—I prize.

Sing, happy soul, thy songs of joy;
Such as a Brook sings in the wood,
That all night has been strengthened by
Heaven's purer flood.

ALE

Now do I hear thee weep and groan,
Who hath a comrade sunk at sea?
Then quaff thee of my good old ale,
And it will raise him up for thee;
Thoul't think as little of him then
As when he moved with living men.

If thou hast hopes to move the world,
And every effort it doth fail,
Then to thy side call Jack and Jim,
And bid them drink with thee good ale;
So may the world, that would not hear,
Perish in hell with all your care.

One quart of good ale, and I
Feel then what life immortal is:
The brain is empty of all thought,
The heart is brimming o'er with bliss;
Time's first child, Life, doth live; but Death,
The second, hath not yet his breath.

Give me a quart of good old ale,
Am I a homeless man on earth?
Nay, I want not your roof and quilt,
I'll lie warm at the moon's cold hearth;
No grumbling ghost to grudge my bed,
His grave, ha! ha! holds up my head.

THE MOON

Thy beauty haunts me heart and soul,
Oh, thou fair Moon, so close and bright;
Thy beauty makes me like the child
That cries aloud to own thy light:
The little child that lifts each arm
To press thee to her bosom warm.

Though there are birds that sing this night
With thy white beams across their throats,
Let my deep silence speak for me
More than for them their sweetest notes:
Who worships thee till music fails,
Is greater than thy nightingales.

NELL BARNES

They lived apart for three long years,
Bill Barnes and Nell his wife;
He took his joy from other girls,
She led a wicked life.

Yet oft times she would pass his shop,
With some strange man awhile;
And, looking, meet her husband's frown
With her malicious smile.

Until one day, when passing there,
She saw her man had gone;
And when she saw the empty shop,
She fell down with a moan.

And when she heard that he had gone
Five thousand miles away;
And that she's see his face no more,
She sickened from that day.

To see his face was health and life,
And when it was denied,
She could not eat, and broke her heart—
It was for love she died.

THE EXAMPLE

Here's an example from
A Butterfly;
That on a rough, hard rock
Happy can lie;
Friendless and all alone
On this unsweetened stone.

Now let my bed be hard
No care take I;
I'll make my joy like this
Small Butterfly;
Whose happy heart has power
To make a stone a flower.

IN MAY

Yes, I will spend the livelong day
With Nature in this month of May;
And sit beneath the trees, and share
My bread with birds whose homes are there;
While cows lie down to eat, and sheep

Stand to their necks in grass so deep;
While birds do sing with all their might,
As though they felt the earth in flight.
This is the hour I dreamed of, when
I sat surrounded by poor men;
And thought of how the Arab sat
Alone at evening, gazing at
The stars that bubbled in clear skies;

And of young dreamers, when their eyes
Enjoyed methought a precious boon
In the adventures of the Moon
Whose light, behind the Clouds' dark bars,
Searched for her stolen flocks of stars.
When I, hemmed in by wrecks of men,
Thought of some lonely cottage then
Full of sweet books; and miles of sea,
With passing ships, in front of me;
And having, on the other hand,
A flowery, green, bird-singing land.

SADNESS AND JOY

I pray you, Sadness, leave me soon,
In sweet invention thou art poor!
Thy sister, Joy can make ten songs
While thou art making four.

One hour with thee is sweet enough;
But when we find the whole day gone
And no created thing is left—
We mourn the evil done.

Thou art too slow to shape thy thoughts
In stone, on canvas, or in song;
But Joy, being full of active heat,
Must do some deed ere long.

Thy sighs are gentle, sweet thy tears;
But if thou canst not help a man
To prove in substance what he feels—
Then give me Joy, who can.

Therefore sweet Sadness, leave me soon,
Let thy bright sister, Joy, come more;
For she can make ten lovely songs

While thou art making four.

DAYS TOO SHORT

When primroses are out in Spring,
And small, blue violets come between;
When merry birds sing on boughs green,
And rills, as soon as born, must sing;

When butterflies will make side-leaps,
As though escaped from Nature's hand
Ere perfect quite; and bees will stand
Upon their heads in fragrant deeps;

When small clouds are so silvery white
Each seems a broken rimmed moon--
When such things are, this world too soon,
For me, doth wear the veil of night.

A GREETING

Good morning, Life—and all
Things glad and beautiful.
My pockets nothing hold,
But he that owns the gold,
The Sun, is my great friend—
His spending has no end.

Hail to the morning sky,
Which bright clouds measure high;
Hail to you birds whose throats
Would number leaves by notes;
Hail to you shady bowers,
And you green field of flowers.

Hail to you women fair,
That make a show so rare
In cloth as white as milk—
Be't calico or silk:
Good morning, Life—and all
Things glad and beautiful.

ALL IN JUNE

A week ago I had a fire
To warm my feet, my hands and face;
Cold winds, that never make a friend,
Crept in and out of every place.

Today the fields are rich in grass,
And buttercups in thousands grow;
I'll show the world where I have been—
With gold-dust seen on either shoe.

Till to my garden back I come,
Where bumble-bees for hours and hours
Sit on their soft, fat, velvet bums,
To wriggle out of hollow flowers.

CHARMS

She walks as lightly as the fly
Skates on the water in July.

To hear her moving petticoat
For me is music's highest note.

Stones are not heard, when her feet pass,
No more than tumps of moss or grass.

When she sits still, she's like the flower
To be a butterfly next hour.

The brook laughs not more sweet, when he
Trips over pebbles suddenly.
My Love, like him, can whisper low—
When he comes where green cresses grow.

She rises like the lark, that hour
He goes halfway to meet a shower.

A fresher drink is in her looks
Than Nature gives me, or old books.

When I in my Love's shadow sit,
I do not miss the sun one bit.

When she is near, my arms can hold

All that's worth having in this world.

And when I know not where she is,
Nothing can come but comes amiss.

THE RAIN

I hear leaves drinking rain;
I hear rich leaves on top
Giving the poor beneath
Drop after drop;
'Tis a sweet noise to hear
These green leaves drinking near.

And when the Sun comes out,
After this Rain shall stop,
A wondrous Light will fill
Each dark, round drop;
I hope the Sun shines bright;
'Twill be a lovely sight.

THE VILLAIN

While joy gave clouds the light of stars,
That beamed wher'er they looked;
And calves and lambs had tottering knees,
Excited, while they sucked;
While every bird enjoyed his song,
Without one thought of harm or wrong—
I turned my head and saw the wind,
Not far from where I stood,
Dragging the corn by her golden hair,
Into a dark and lonely wood.

THE KINGFISHER

It was the Rainbow gave thee birth,
And left thee all her lovely hues;
And, as her mother's name was Tears,
So runs it in my blood to choose
For haunts the lonely pools, and keep
In company with trees that weep.

Go you and, with such glorious hues,
Live with proud peacocks in green parks;
On lawns as smooth as shining glass,
Let every feather show its marks;
Get thee on boughs and clap thy wings
Before the windows of proud kings.
Nay, lovely Bird, thou art not vain;
Thou hast no proud, ambitious mind;
I also love a quiet place
That's green, away from all mankind;
A lonely pool, and let a tree
Sigh with her bosom over me.

NO MASTER

Indeed this is the sweet life! my hand
Is under no proud man's command;
There is no voice to break my rest
Before a bird has left its nest;
There is no man to change my mood,
When I go nutting in the wood;
No man to pluck my sleeve and say—
I want thy labour for this day;
No man to keep me out of sight,
When that dear Sun is shining bright.
None but my friends shall have command
Upon my time, my heart and hand;
I'll rise from sleep to help a friend,
But let no stranger orders send,
Or hear my curses fast and thick,
Which in his purse-proud throat would stick
Like burrs. If I cannot be free
To do such work as pleases me,
Near woodland pools and under trees,
You'll get no work at all, for I
Would rather live this life and die
A beggar or a thief, than be
A working slave with no days free.

COME, LET US FIND

Come, let us find a cottage, love,
That's green for half a mile around;
To laugh at every grumbling bee,

Whose sweetest blossom's not yet found.
Where many a bird shall sing for you,
And in your garden build its nest:
They'll sing for you as though their eggs
Were lying in your breast,
My love--
Were lying warm in your soft breast.

'Tis strange how men find time to hate,
When life is all too short for love;
But we, away from our own kind,
A different life can live and prove.
And early on a summer's morn,
As I go walking out with you,
We'll help the sun with our warm breath
To clear away the dew,
My love,
To clear away the morning dew.

A GREAT TIME

Sweet Chance, that led my steps abroad,
Beyond the town, where wild flowers grow—
A rainbow and a cuckoo, Lord,
How rich and great the times are now!
Know, all ye sheep
And cows, that keep
On staring that I stand so long
In grass that's wet from heavy rain—
A rainbow and a cuckoo's song
May never come together again;
May never come
This side the tomb.

A FLEETING PASSION

Thou shalt not laugh, thou shalt not romp,
Let's grimly kiss with bated breath;
As quietly and solemnly
As Life when it is kissing Death.
Now in the silence of the grave,
My hand is squeezing that soft breast;
While thou dost in such passion lie,
It mocks me with its look of rest.

But when the morning comes at last,
And we must part, our passions cold,
You'll think of some new feather, scarf
To buy with my small piece of gold;
And I'll be dreaming of green lanes,
Where little things with beating hearts
Hold shining eyes between the leaves,
Till men with horses pass, and carts.

IN THE COUNTRY

This life is sweetest; in this wood
I hear no children cry for food;
I see no woman, white with care;
No man, with muscled wasting here.

No doubt it is a selfish thing
To fly from human suffering;
No doubt he is a selfish man,
Who shuns poor creatures, sad and wan.

But 'tis a wretched life to face
Hunger in almost every place;
Cursed with a hand that's empty, when
The heart is full to help all men.

Can I admire the statue great,
When living men starve at its feet!
Can I admire the park's green tree,
A roof for homeless misery!

APRIL'S CHARMS

When April scatters charms of primrose gold
Among the copper leaves in thickets old,
And singing skylarks from the meadows rise,
To twinkle like black stars in sunny skies;

When I can hear the small woodpecker ring
Time on a tree for all the birds that sing;
And hear the pleasant cuckoo, loud and long—
The simple bird that thinks two notes a song;

When I can hear the woodland brook, that could
Not drown a babe, with all his threatening mood;
Upon these banks the violets make their home,
And let a few small strawberry blossoms come:

When I go forth on such a pleasant day,
One breath outdoors takes all my cares away;
It goes like heavy smoke, when flames take hold
Of wood that's green and fill a grate with gold.

RICH OR POOR

With thy true love I have more wealth
Than Charon's piled-up bank doth hold;
Where he makes kings lay down their crowns
And life-long misers leave their gold.

Without thy love I've no more wealth
Than seen upon that other shore;
That cold, bare bank he rows them to—
Those kings and misers made so poor.

THE BEST FRIEND

Now shall I walk
Or shall I ride?
"Ride", Pleasure said;
"Walk", Joy replied.

Now what shall I—
Stay home or roam?
"Roam", Pleasure said;
And Joy—"stay home."

Now shall I dance,
Or sit for dreams?
"Sit," answers Joy;
"Dance," Pleasure screams.

Which of ye two
Will kindest be?
Pleasure laughed sweet,
But Joy kissed me.

A PLAIN LIFE

No idle gold—since this fine sun, my friend,
Is no mean miser, but doth freely spend.

No prescious stones—since these green mornings show,
Without a charge, their pearls where'er I go.

No lifeless books—since birds with their sweet tongues
Will read aloud to me their happier songs.

No painted scenes—since clouds can change their skies
A hundred times a day to please my eyes.

No headstrong wine—since, when I drink, the spring
Into my eager ears will softly sing.

No surplus clothes—since every simple beast
Can teach me to be happy with the least.

JOY AND PLEASURE

Now, joy is born of parents poor,
And pleasure of our richer kind;
Though pleasure's free, she cannot sing
As sweet a song as joy confined.

Pleasure's a Moth, that sleeps by day
And dances by false glare at night;
But Joy's a Butterfly, that loves
To spread its wings in Nature's light.

Joy's like a Bee that gently sucks
Away on blossoms its sweet hour;
But pleasure's like a greedy Wasp,
That plums and cherries would devour.

Joy's like a Lark that lives alone,
Whose ties are very strong, though few;
But Pleasure like a Cuckoo roams,
Makes much acquaintance, no friends true.

Joy from her heart doth sing at home,
With little care if others hear;

But pleasure then is cold and dumb,
And sings and laughs with strangers near.

MONEY

When I had money, money, O!
I knew no joy till I went poor;
For many a false man as a friend
Came knocking all day at my door.
Then felt I like a child that holds
A trumpet that he must not blow
Because a man is dead; I dared
Not speak to let this false world know.
Much have I thought of life, and seen
How poor men's hearts are ever light;
And how their wives do hum like bees
About their work from morn till night.
So, when I hear these poor ones laugh,
And see the rich ones coldly frown—
Poor men, think I, need not go up
So much as rich men should come down.
When I had money, money, O!
My many friends proved all untrue;
But now I have no money, O!
My friends are real, though very few.

LEISURE

What is this life if, full of care,
We have no time to stand and stare?—

No time to stand beneath the boughs,
And stare as long as sheep and cows:

No time to see, when woods we pass,
Where squirrels hide their nuts in grass:

No time to see, in broad daylight,
Streams full of stars, like skies at night:

No time to turn at Beauty's glance,
And watch her feet, how they can dance:

No time to wait till her mouth can
Enrich that smile her eyes began?

A poor life this if, full of care,
We have no time to stand and stare.

THUNDERSTORMS

My mind has thunderstorms,
That brood for heavy hours:
Until they rain me words,
My thoughts are drooping flowers
And sulking, silent birds.

Yet come, dark thunderstorms,
And brood your heavy hours;
For when you rain me words,
My thoughts are dancing flowers
And joyful singing birds.

STRONG MOMENTS

Sometimes I hear fine ladies sing,
Sometimes I smoke and drink with men;
Sometimes I play at games of cards—
Judge me to be no strong man then.

The strongest moment of my life
Is when I think about the poor;
When, like a spring that rain has fed,
My pity rises more and more.

The flower that loves the warmth and light,
Has all its mornings bathed in dew;
My heart has moments wet with tears,
My weakness is they are so few.

A GREETING

Good morning, Life—and all
Things glad and beautiful.
My pockets nothing hold,
But he that owns the gold,
The Sun, is my great friend—
His spending has no end.

Hail to the morning sky,
Which bright clouds measure high;
Hail to you birds whose throats
Would number leaves by notes;
Hail to you shady bowers,
And you green fields of flowers.

Hail to you women fair,
That make a show so rare
In cloth as white as milk—
Be't calico or silk:
Good morning, Life—and all
Things glad and beautiful.

SWEET STAY-AT-HOME

Sweet Stay-at-Home, sweet Well-content,
Thou knowest of no strange continent:
Thou hast not felt thy bosom keep
A gentle motion with the deep;
Thou hast not sailed in Indian seas,
Where scent comes forth in every breeze.
Thou hast not seen the rich grape grow
For miles, as far as eyes can go;
Thou hast not seen a summer's night
When maids could sew by a worm's light;
Nor the North Sea in spring send out
Bright hues that like birds flit about
In solid cages of white ice—
Sweet Stay-at-Home, sweet Love-one-place.
Thou hast not seen black fingers pick
White cotton when the bloom is thick,
Nor heard black throats in harmony;
Nor hast thou sat on stones that lie
Flat on the earth, that once did rise
To hide proud kings from common eyes,
Thou hast not seen plains full of bloom
Where green things had such little room
They pleased the eye like fairer flowers—
Sweet Stay-at-Home, all these long hours.
Sweet Well-content, sweet Love-one-place,
Sweet, simple maid, bless thy dear face;
For thou hast made more homely stuff
Nurture thy gentle self enough;
I love thee for a heart that's kind—

Not for the knowledge in thy mind.

THE STARVED

My little Lamb, what is amiss?
If there was milk in mother's kiss,
You would not look as white as this.

The wolf of Hunger, it is he
That takes away thy milk from me,
And I have much to do for thee.

If thou couldst live on love, I know
No babe in all the land could show
More rosy cheeks and louder crow.

Thy father's dead, Alas for thee:
I cannot keep this wolf from me,
That takes thy milk so bold and free.

If thy dear father lived, he'd drive
Away this beast with whom I strive,
And thou, my pretty Lamb, wouldst thrive.

Ah, my poor babe, my love's so great
I'd swallow common rags for meat—
If they could make milk rich and sweet.

My little Lamb, what is amiss?
Come, I must wake thee with a kiss,
For Death would own a sleep like this.

A MAY MORNING

The sky is clear,
The sun is bright;
The cows are red,
The sheep are white;
Trees in the meadows
Make happy shadows.

Birds in the hedge
Are perched and sing;
Swallows and larks

Are on the wing:
Two merry cuckoos
Are making echoes.

Bird and the beast
Have the dew yet;
My road shines dry,
Theirs bright and wet:
Death gives no warning,
On this May morning.

I see no Christ
Nailed on a tree,
Dying for sin;
No sin I see:
No thoughts for sadness,
All thoughts for gladness.

THE LONELY DREAMER

He lives his lonely life, and when he dies
A thousand hearts maybe will utter sighs;
Because they liked his songs, and now their bird
Sleeps with his head beneath his wing, unheard.

But what kind hand will tend his grave, and bring
Those blossoms there, of which he used to sing?
Who'll kiss his mound, and wish the time would come
To lie with him inside that silent tomb?

And who'll forget the dreamer's skill, and shed
A tear because a loving heart is dead?
Heigh ho for gossip then, and common sighs--
And let his death bring tears in no one's eyes.

CHRISTMAS

Christmas has come, let's eat and drink—
This is no time to sit and think;
Farewell to study, books and pen,
And welcome to all kinds of men.
Let all men now get rid of care,
And what one has let others share;
Then 'tis the same, no matter which

Of us is poor, or which is rich.
Let each man have enough this day,
Since those that can are glad to pay;
There's nothing now too rich or good
For poor men, not the King's own food.
Now like a singing bird my feet
Touch earth, and I must drink and eat.
Welcome to all men: I'll not care
What any of my fellows wear;
We'll not let cloth divide our souls,
They'll swim stark naked in the bowls.
Welcome, poor beggar: I'll not see
That hand of yours dislodge a flea, —
While you sit at my side and beg,
Or right foot scratching your left leg.
Farewell restraint: we will not now
Measure the ale our brains allow,
But drink as much as we can hold.
We'll count no change when we spend gold;
This is no time to save, but spend,
To give for nothing, not to lend.
Let foes make friends: let them forget
The mischief-making dead that fret
The living with complaint like this—
"He wronged us once, hate him and his."
Christmas has come; let every man
Eat, drink, be merry all he can.
Ale's my best mark, but if port wine
Or whisky's yours—let it be mine;
No matter what lies in the bowls,
We'll make it rich with our own souls.
Farewell to study, books and pen,
And welcome to all kinds of men.

LAUGHING ROSE

If I were gusty April now,
How I would blow at laughing Rose;
I'd make her ribbons slip their knots,
And all her hair come loose.

If I were merry April now,
How I would pelt her cheeks with showers;
I'd make carnations, rich and warm,
Of her vermilion flowers.

Since she will laugh in April's face,
No matter how he rains or blows—
Then O that I wild April were,
To play with laughing Rose.

SEEKING JOY

Joy, how I sought thee!
Silver I spent and gold,
On the pleasures of this world,
In splendid garments clad;
The wine I drank was sweet,
Rich morsels I did eat—
Oh, but my life was sad!
Joy, how I sought thee!

Joy, I have found thee!
Far from the halls of Mirth,
Back to the soft green earth,
Where people are not many;
I find thee, Joy, in hours
With clouds, and birds, and flowers—
Thou dost not charge one penny.
Joy, I have found thee!

THE OLD OAK TREE

I sit beneath your leaves, old oak,
You mighty one of all the trees;
Within whose hollow trunk a man
Could stable his big horse with ease.

I see your knuckles hard and strong,
But have no fear they'll come to blows;
Your life is long, and mine is short,
But which has known the greater woes?

Thou has not seen starved women here,
Or man gone mad because ill-fed—
Who stares at stones in city streets,
Mistaking them for hunks of bread.

Thou hast not felt the shivering backs
Of homeless children lying down

And sleeping in the cold, night air—
Like doors and walls in London town.

Knowing thou hast not known such shame,
And only storms have come thy way,
Methinks I could in comfort spend
My summer with thee, day by day.

To lie by day in thy green shade,
And in thy hollow rest at night;
And through the open doorway see
The stars turn over leaves of light.

POOR KINGS

God's pity on poor kings,
They know no gentle rest;
The North and South cry out,
Cries come from East and West—
"Come, open this new Dock,
Building, Bazaar or Fair."
Lord, what a wretched life
Such men must bear.

They're followed, watched and spied,
No liberty they know;
Some eye will watch them still,
No matter where they go.
When in green lanes I muse,
Alone, and hear birds sing,
God's pity then, say I,
On some poor king.

LOVE AND THE MUSE

My back is turned on Spring and all her flowers,
The birds no longer charm from tree to tree;
The cuckoo had his home in this green world
Ten days before his voice was heard by me.

Had I an answer from a dear one's lips,
My love of life would soon regain its power;
And suckle my sweet dreams, that tug my heart,
And whimper to be nourished every hour.

Give me that answer now, and then my Muse,
That for my sweet life's sake must never die,
Will rise like that great wave that leaps and hangs
The sea-weed on a vessel's mast-top high.

MY YOUTH

My youth was my old age,
Weary and long;
It had too many cares
To think of song;
My moulting days all came
When I was young.

Now, in life's prime, my soul
Comes out in flower;
Late, as with Robin, comes
My singing power;
I was not born to joy
Till this late hour.

SMILES

I saw a black girl once,
As black as winter's night;
Till through her parted lips
There came a flood of light;
It was the milky way
Across her face so black:
Her two lips closed again,
And night came back.

I see a maiden now,
Fair as a summer's day;
Yet through her parted lips
I see the milky way;
It makes the broad daylight
In summer time look black:
Her two lips close again,
And night comes back.

MAD POLL

There goes mad Poll, dressed in wild flowers,
Poor, crazy Poll, now old and wan;
Her hair all down, like any child:
She swings her two arms like a man.

Poor, crazy Poll is never sad,
She never misses one that dies;
When neighbours show their new-born babes,
They seem familiar to her eyes.

Her bonnet's always in her hand,
Or on the ground, and lying near;
She thinks it is a thing for play,
Or pretty show, and not to wear.

She gives the sick no sympathy,
She never soothes a child that cries;
She never whimpers, night or day,
She makes no moans, she makes no sighs.

She talks about some battle old,
Fought many a day from yesterday;
And when that war is done, her love—
"Ha, ha!" Poll laughs, and skips away.

JOY SUPREME

The birds are pirates of her notes,
The blossoms steal her face's light;
The stars in ambush lie all day,
To take her glances for the night.
Her voice can shame rain-pelted leaves;
Young robin has no notes as sweet
In autumn, when the air is still,
And all the other birds are mute.

When I set eyes on ripe, red plums
That seem a sin and shame to bite,
Such are her lips, which I would kiss,
And still would keep before my sight.
When I behold proud gossamer
Make silent billows in the air,
Then think I of her head's fine stuff,
Finer than gossamer's, I swear.

The miser has his joy, with gold
Beneath his pillow in the night;
My head shall lie on soft warm hair,
And miser's know not that delight.
Captains that own their ships can boast
Their joy to feel the rolling brine—
But I shall lie near her, and feel
Her soft warm bosom swell on mine.

FRANCIS THOMPSON

Thou hadst no home, and thou couldst see
In every street the windows' light:
Dragging thy limbs about all night,
No window kept a light for thee.

However much thou wert distressed,
Or tired of moving, and felt sick,
Thy life was on the open deck—
Thou hadst no cabin for thy rest.

Thy barque was helpless 'neath the sky,
No pilot thought thee worth his pains
To guide for love or money gains—
Like phantom ships the rich sailed by.

Thy shadow mocked thee night and day,
Thy life's companion, it alone;
It did not sigh, it did not moan,
But mocked thy moves in every way.

In spite of all, the mind had force,
And, like a stream whose surface flows
The wrong way when a strong wind blows,
It underneath maintained its course.

Oft didst thou think thy mind would flower
Too late for good, as some bruised tree
That blooms in Autumn, and we see
Fruit not worth picking, hard and sour.

Some poets feign their wounds and scars.
If they had known real suffering hours,
They'd show, in place of Fancy's flowers,
More of Imagination's stars.

So, if thy fruits of Poesy
Are rich, it is at this dear cost—
That they were nipt by Sorrow's frost,
In nights of homeless misery.

THE BIRD-MAN

Man is a bird:
He rises on fine wings
Into the Heaven's clear light;
He flies away and sings—
There's music in his flight.

Man is a bird:
In swiftest speed he burns,
With twist and dive and leap;
A bird whose sudden turns
Can drive the frightened sheep.

Man is a bird:
Over the mountain high,
Whose head is in the skies,
Cut from its shoulder by
A cloud—the bird-man flies.

Man is a bird:
Eagles from mountain crag
Swooped down to prove his worth;
But now they rise to drag
Him down from Heaven to earth!

WINTER'S BEAUTY

Is it not fine to walk in spring,
When leaves are born, and hear birds sing?
And when they lose their singing powers,
In summer, watch the bees at flowers?
Is it not fine, when summer's past,
To have the leaves, no longer fast,
Biting my heel where'er I go,
Or dancing lightly on my toe?
Now winter's here and rivers freeze;
As I walk out I see the trees,

Wherein the pretty squirrels sleep,
All standing in the snow so deep:
And every twig, however small,
Is blossomed white and beautiful.
Then welcome, winter, with thy power
To make this tree a big white flower;
To make this tree a lovely sight,
With fifty brown arms draped in white,
While thousands of small fingers show
In soft white gloves of purest snow.

THE CHURCH ORGAN

The homeless man has heard thy voice,
Its sound doth move his memory deep;
He stares bewildered, as a man
That's shook by earthquake in his sleep.

Thy solemn voice doth bring to mind
The days that are forever gone:
Thou bringest to mind our early days,
Ere we made second homes or none.

HEIGH HO, THE RAIN

The Lark that in heaven dim
Can match a rainy hour
With his own music's shower,
Can make me sing like him—
Heigh ho! The rain!

Sing--when a Nightingale
Pours forth her own sweet soul
To hear dread thunder roll
Into a tearful tale—
Heigh ho! The rain!

Sing--when a Sparrow's seen
Trying to lie at rest
By pressing his warm breast
To leaves so wet and green—
Heigh ho! The rain!

LOVE'S INSPIRATION

Give me the chance, and I will make
Thy thoughts of me, like worms this day,
Take wings and change to butterflies
That in the golden light shall play;
Thy cold, clear heart--the quiet pool
That never heard Love's nightingale—
Shall hear his music night and day,
And in no seasons shall it fail.

I'll make thy happy heart my port,
Where all my thoughts are anchored fast;
Thy meditations, full of praise,
The flags of glory on each mast.
I'll make my Soul thy shepherd soon,
With all thy thoughts my grateful flock;
And thou shalt say, each time I go—
How long, my Love, ere thou'lt come back?

NIGHT WANDERERS

They hear the bell of midnight toll,
And shiver in their flesh and soul;
They lie on hard, cold wood or stone,
Iron, and ache in every bone;
They hate the night: they see no eyes
Of loved ones in the starlit skies.
They see the cold, dark water near;
They dare not take long looks for fear
They'll fall like those poor birds that see
A snake's eyes staring at their tree.
Some of them laugh, half-mad; and some
All through the chilly night are dumb;
Like poor, weak infants some converse,
And cough like giants, deep and hoarse.

YOUNG BEAUTY

When at each door the ruffian winds
Have laid a dying man to groan,
And filled the air on winter nights
With cries of infants left alone;

And every thing that has a bed
Will sigh for others that have none:

On such a night, when bitter cold,
Young Beauty, full of love thoughts sweet,
Can redden in her looking-glass;
With but one gown on, in bare feet,
She from her own reflected charms
Can feel the joy of summer's heat.

WHO I KNOW

I do not know his grace the Duke,
Outside whose gilded gate there died
Of want a feeble, poor old man,
With but his shadow at his side.

I do not know his Lady fair,
Who in a bath of milk doth lie;
More milk than could feed fifty babes,
That for the want of it must die.

But well I know the mother poor,
Three pounds of flesh wrapped in her shawl:
A puny babe that, stripped at home,
Looks like a rabbit skinned, so small.

And well I know the homeless waif,
Fed by the poorest of the poor;
Since I have seen that child alone,
Crying against a bolted door.

SWEET BIRDS, I COME

The bird that now
On bush and tree,
Near leaves so green
Looks down to see
Flowers looking up—
He either sings
In ecstasy
Or claps his wings.

Why should I slave

For finer dress
Or ornaments;
Will flowers smile less
For rags than silk?
Are birds less dumb
For tramp than squire?
Sweet birds, I come.

THE TWO LIVES

Now how could I, with gold to spare,
Who know the harlot's arms, and wine,
Sit in this green field all alone,
If Nature was not truly mine?

That Pleasure life wakes stale at morn,
From heavy sleep that no rest brings:
This life of quiet joy wakes fresh,
And claps its wings at morn, and sings.

So here sit I, alone till noon,
In one long dream of quiet bliss;
I hear the lark and share his joy,
With no more winedrops than were his.

Such, Nature, is thy charm and power—
Since I have made the Muse my wife—
To keep me from the harlot's arms,
And save me from a drunkard's life.

HIDDEN LOVE

The bird of Fortune sings when free,
But captured, soon grows dumb; and we,
To hear his fast declining powers,
Must soon forget that he is ours.
So, when I win that maid, no doubt
Love soon will seem to be half out;
Like blighted leaves drooped to the ground,
Whose roots are still untouched and sound,
So will our love's root still be strong
When others think the leaves go wrong.
Though we may quarrel, 'twill not prove
That she and I are less in love;

The parrot, though he mocked the dove,
Died when she died, and proved his love.
When merry springtime comes, we hear
How all things into love must stir;
How birds would rather sing than eat,
How joyful sheep would rather bleat:
And daffodils nod heads of gold,
And dance in April's sparkling cold.
So in our early love did we
Dance much and skip, and laugh with glee:
But let none think our love is flown
If, when we're married, little's shown:
E'en though our lips be dumb of song,
Our hearts can still be singing strong.

LIFE IS JOLLY

This life is jolly, O!
I envy no man's lot;
My eyes can much admire,
And still my heart crave not;
There's no true joy in gold,
It breeds desire for more;
Whatever wealth man has,
Desire can keep him poor.

This life is jolly, O!
Power has his fawning slaves,
But if he rests his mind,
Those wretches turn bold knaves.
Fame's field is full of flowers,
It dazzles as we pass,
But men who walk that field
Starve for the common grass.

This life is jolly, O!
Let others know they die,
Enough to know I live,
And make no question why;
I care not whence I came,
Nor whither I shall go;
Let others think of these—
This life is jolly, O!

THE FOG

I saw the fog grow thick,
Which soon made blind my ken;
It made tall men of boys,
And giants of tall men.

It clutched my throat, I coughed;
Nothing was in my head
Except two heavy eyes
Like balls of burning lead.

And when it grew so black
That I could know no place,
I lost all judgment then,
Of distance and of space.

The street lamps, and the lights
Upon the halted cars,
Could either be on earth
Or be the heavenly stars.

A man passed by me close,
I asked my way, he said,
"Come, follow me, my friend"
I followed where he led.

He rapped the stones in front,
"Trust me," he said, "and come";
I followed like a child—
A blind man led me home.

A WOMAN'S CHARMS

My purse is yours, Sweet Heart, for I
Can count no coins with you close by;
I scorn like sailors them, when they
Have drawn on shore their deep-sea pay;
Only my thoughts I value now,
Which, like the simple glowworms, throw
Their beams to greet thee bravely, Love
Their glorious light in Heaven above.
Since I have felt thy waves of light,
Beating against my soul, the sight
Of gems from Afric's continent
Move me to no great wonderment.

Since I, Sweet Heart, have known thine hair,
The fur of ermine, sable, bear,
Or silver fox, for me can keep
No more to praise than common sheep.
Though ten Isaiahs' souls were mine,
They could not sing such charms as thine.
Two little hands that show with pride,
Two timid, little feet that hide;
Two eyes no dark Senoras show
Their burning like in Mexico;
Two coral gates wherein is shown
Your queen of charms, on a white throne;
Your queen of charms, the lovely smile
That on its white throne could beguile
The mastiff from his gates in hell;
Who by no whine or bark could tell
His masters what thing made him go—
And countless other charms I know.
October's hedge has far less hues
Than thou hast charms from which to choose.

DREAMS OF THE SEA

I know not why I yearn for thee again,
To sail once more upon thy fickle flood;
I'll hear thy waves wash under my death-bed,
Thy salt is lodged forever in my blood.

Yet I have seen thee lash the vessel's sides
In fury, with thy many tailed whip;
And I have seen thee, too, like Galilee,
When Jesus walked in peace to Simon's ship

And I have seen thy gentle breeze as soft
As summer's, when it makes the cornfields run;
And I have seen thy rude and lusty gale
Make ships show half their bellies to the sun.

Thou knowest the way to tame the wildest life,
Thou knowest the way to bend the great and proud:
I think of that Armada whose puffed sails,
Greedy and large, came swallowing every cloud.

But I have seen the sea-boy, young and drowned,
Lying on shore and by thy cruel hand,
A seaweed beard was on his tender chin,

His heaven-blue eyes were filled with common sand.

And yet, for all, I yearn for thee again,
To sail once more upon thy fickle flood:
I'll hear thy waves wash under my death-bed,
Thy salt is lodged forever in my blood.

THE WONDER MAKER

Come, if thou'rt cold to Summer's charms,
Her clouds of green, her starry flowers,
And let this bird, this wandering bird,
Make his fine wonder yours;
He, hiding in the leaves so green,
When sampling this fair world of ours,
Cries cuckoo, clear; and like Lot's wife,
I look, though it should cost my life.

When I can hear that charmed one's voice,
I taste of immortality;
My joy's so great that on my heart
Doth lie eternity,
As light as any little flower—
So strong a wonder works in me;
Cuckoo! he cries, and fills my soul
With all that's rich and beautiful.

THE HELPLESS

Those poor, heartbroken wretches, doomed
To hear at night the clocks' hard tones;
They have no beds to warm their limbs,
But with those limbs must warm cold stones;
Those poor weak men, whose coughs and ailings
Force them to tear at iron railings.

Those helpless men that starve, my pity;
Whose waking day is never done;
Who, save for their own shadows, are
Doomed night and day to walk alone:
They know no bright face but the sun's,
So cold and dark are human ones.

AN EARLY LOVE

Ah, sweet young blood, that makes the heart
So full of joy, and light,
That dying children dance with it
From early morn till night.

My dreams were blossoms, hers the fruit,
She was my dearest care;
With gentle hand, and for it, I
Made playthings of her hair.

I made my fingers rings of gold,
And bangles for my wrist;
You should have felt the soft, warm thing
I made to glove my fist.

And she should have a crown, I swore,
With only gold enough
To keep together stones more rich
Than that fine metal stuff.

Her golden hair gave me more joy
Than Jason's heart could hold,
When all his men cried out—Ah, look!
He has the Fleece of Gold!

DREAM TRAGEDIES

Thou art not always kind, O sleep:
What awful secrets them dost keep
In store, and oft times make us know;
What hero has not fallen low
In sleep before a monster grim,
And whined for mercy unto him;
Knights, constables, and men-at-arms
Have quailed and whined in sleep's alarms.
Thou wert not kind last night to make
Me like a very coward shake—
Shake like a thin red-currant bush
Robbed of its fruit by a strong thrush.
I felt this earth did move; more slow,
And slower yet began to go;
And not a bird was heard to sing,
Men and great beasts were shivering;

All living things knew well that when
This earth stood still, destruction then
Would follow with a mighty crash.
'Twas then I broke that awful hush:
E'en as a mother, who does come
Running in haste back to her home,
And looks at once, and lo, the child
She left asleep is gone; and wild
She shrieks and loud—so did I break
With a mad cry that dream, and wake.

CHILDREN AT PLAY

I hear a merry noise indeed:
Is it the geese and ducks that take
Their first plunge in a quiet pond
That into scores of ripples break—
Or children make this merry sound?

I see an oak tree, its strong back
Could not be bent an inch though all
Its leaves were stone, or iron even:
A boy, with many a lusty call,
Rides on a bough bareback through Heaven.

I see two children dig a hole
And plant in it a cherry-stone:
"We'll come to-morrow," one child said—
"And then the tree will be full grown,
And all its boughs have cherries red."

Ah, children, what a life to lead:
You love the flowers, but when they're past
No flowers are missed by your bright eyes;
And when cold winter comes at last,
Snowflakes shall be your butterflies.

WHEN THE CUCKOO SINGS

In summer, when the Cuckoo sings,
And clouds like greater moons can shine;
When every leafy tree doth hold
A loving heart that beats with mine:
Now, when the Brook has cresses green,

As well as stones, to check his pace;
And, if the Owl appears, he's forced
By small birds to some hiding-place:
Then, like red Robin in the spring,
I shun those haunts where men are found;
My house holds little joy until
Leaves fall and birds can make no sound;
Let none invade that wilderness
Into whose dark green depths I go—
Save some fine lady, all in white,
Comes like a pillar of pure snow.

RETURN TO NATURE

My song is of that city which
Has men too poor and men too rich;
Where some are sick, too richly fed,
While others take the sparrows' bread:
Where some have beds to warm their bones,
While others sleep on hard, cold stones
That suck away their bodies' heat.
Where men are drunk in every street;
Men full of poison, like those flies
That still attack the horses' eyes.
Where some men freeze for want of cloth,
While others show their jewels' worth
And dress in satin, fur or silk;
Where fine rich ladies wash in milk,
While starving mothers have no food
To make them fit in flesh and blood;
So that their watery breasts can give
Their babies milk and make them live.
Where one man does the work of four,
And dies worn out before his hour;
While some seek work in vain, and grief
Doth make their fretful lives as brief.
Where ragged men are seen to wait
For charity that's small and late;
While others haunt in idle leisure,
Theatre doors to pay for pleasure.
No more I'll walk those crowded places
And take hot dreams from harlots' faces;
I'll know no more those passions' dreams,
While musing near these quiet streams;
That biting state of savage lust
Which, true love absent, burns to dust.

Gold's rattle shall not rob my ears
Of this sweet music of the spheres.
I'll walk abroad with fancy free;
Each leafy, summer's morn I'll see
The trees, all legs or bodies, when
They vary in their shapes like men.
I'll walk abroad and see again
How quiet pools are pricked by rain;
And you shall hear a song as sweet
As when green leaves and raindrops meet.
I'll hear the Nightingale's fine mood,
Rattling with thunder in the wood,
Made bolder by each mighty crash;
Who drives her notes with every flash
Of lightning through the summer's night.
No more I'll walk in that pale light
That shows the homeless man awake,
Ragged and cold; harlot and rake,
That have their hearts in rags, and die
Before that poor wretch they pass by.
Nay, I have found a life so fine
That every moment seems divine;
By shunning all those pleasures full,
That bring repentance cold and dull.
Such misery seen in days gone by,
That, made a coward, now I fly
To green things, like a bird. Alas!
In days gone by I could not pass
Ten men but what the eyes of one
Would burn me for no kindness done;
And wretched women I passed by
Sent after me a moan or sigh.
Ah, wretched days: for in that place
My soul's leaves sought the human face,
And not the Sun's for warmth and light—
And so was never free from blight.
But seek me now, and you will find
Me on some soft green bank reclined;
Watching the stately deer close by,
That in a great deep hollow lie
Shaking their tails with all the ease
That lambs can. First, look for the trees,
Then, if you seek me, find me quick.
Seek me no more where men are thick,
But in green lanes where I can walk
A mile, and still no human folk
Tread on my shadow. Seek me where
The strange oak tree is, that can bear

One white-leaved branch among the green—
Which many a woodman has not seen.
If you would find me, go where cows
And sheep stand under shady boughs;
Where furious squirrels shake a tree
As though they'd like to bury me
Under a leaf shower heavy, and
I laugh at them for spite, and stand.
Seek me no more in human ways—
Who am a coward since those days
My mind was burned by poor men's eyes,
And frozen by poor women's sighs.
Then send your pearls across the sea,
Your feathers, scent and ivory,
You distant lands--but let my bales
Be brought by Cuckoos, Nightingales,
That come in spring from your far shores;
Sweet birds that carry richer stores
Than men can dream of, when they prize
Fine silks and pearls for merchandise;
And dream of ships that take the floods
Sunk to their decks with such vain goods;
Bringing that traitor silk, whose soft
Smooth tongue persuades the poor too oft
From sweet content; and pearls, whose fires
Make ashes of our best desires.
For I have heard the sighs and whines
Of rich men that drink costly wines
And eat the best of fish and fowl;
Men that have plenty, and still growl
Because they cannot like kings live—
"Alas!" they whine, "we cannot save."
Since I have heard those rich ones sigh,
Made poor by their desires so high,
I cherish more a simple mind;
That I am well content to find
My pictures in the open air,
And let my walls and floors go bare;
That I with lovely things can fill
My rooms, whene'er sweet Fancy will.
I make a fallen tree my chair,
And soon forget no cushion's there;
I lie upon the grass or straw,
And no soft down do I sigh for;
For with me all the time I keep
Sweet dreams that, do I wake or sleep,
Shed on me still their kindly beams;
Aye, I am richer with my dreams

Than banks where men dull-eyed and cold
Without a tremble shovel gold.
A happy life is this. I walk
And hear more birds than people talk;
I hear the birds that sing unseen,
On boughs now smothered with leaves green;
I sit and watch the swallows there,
Making a circus in the air;
That speed around straight-going crow,
As sharks around a ship can go;
I hear the skylark out of sight,
Hid perfectly in all this light.
The dappled cows in fields I pass,
Up to their bosoms in deep grass;
Old oak trees, with their bowels gone,
I see with spring's green finery on.
I watch the buzzing bees for hours,
To see them rush at laughing flowers—
And butterflies that lie so still.
I see great houses on the hill,
With shining roofs; and there shines one,
It seems that heaven has dropped the sun.
I see yon cloudlet sail the skies,
Racing with clouds ten times its size.
I walk green pathways, where love waits
To talk in whispers at old gates;
Past stiles--on which I lean, alone—
Carved with the names of lovers gone;
I stand on arches whose dark stones
Can turn the wind's soft sighs to groans.
I hear the Cuckoo when first he
Makes this green world's discovery,
And re-creates it in my mind,
Proving my eyes were growing blind.
I see the rainbow come forth clear
And wave her coloured scarf to cheer
The sun long swallowed by a flood—
So do I live in lane and wood.
Let me look forward to each spring
As eager as the birds that sing;
And feed my eyes on spring's young flowers
Before the bees by many hours,
My heart to leap and sing her praise
Before the birds by many days.
Go white my hair and skin go dry—
But let my heart a dewdrop lie
Inside those leaves when they go wrong,
As fresh as when my life was young.

A STRANGE CITY

A wondrous city, that had temples there
More rich than that one built by David's son,
Which called forth Ophir's gold, when Israel
Made Lebanon half naked for her sake.
I saw white towers where so-called traitors died—
True men whose tongues were bells to honest hearts,
And rang out boldly in false monarch's ears.
Saw old black gateways, on whose arches crouched
Stone lions with their bodies gnawed by age.
I looked with awe on iron gates that could
Tell bloody stones if they had our tongues.
I saw tall mounted spires shine in the sun,
That stood amidst their army of low streets.
I saw in buildings pictures, statues rare,
Made in those days when Rome was young, and new
In marble quarried from Carrara's hills;
Statues by sculptors that could almost make
Fine cobwebs out of stone--so light they worked.
Pictures that breathe in us a living soul,
Such as we seldom feel come from that life
The artist copies. Many a lovely sight—
Such as the half sunk barge with bales of hay,
Or sparkling coals--employed my wondering eyes.
I saw old Thames, whose ripples swarmed with stars
Bred by the sun on that fine summer's day;
I saw in fancy fowl and green banks there,
And Liza's barge rowed past a thousand swans.
I walked in parks and heard sweet music cry
In solemn courtyards, midst the men-at-arms;
Which suddenly would leap those stony walls
And spring up with loud laughter into trees.
I walked in busy streets where music oft
Went on the march with men; and ofttimes heard
The organ in cathedral, when the boys
Like nightingales sang in that thunderstorm;
The organ, with its rich and solemn tones—
As near a God's voice as a man conceives;
Nor ever dreamt the silent misery
That solemn organ brought to homeless men.
I heard the drums and soft brass instruments,
Led by the silver cornets clear and high—
Whose sounds turned playing children into stones.

I saw at night the City's lights shine bright,
A greater milky way; how in its spell
It fascinated with ten thousand eyes;
Like those sweet wiles of an enchantress who
Would still detain her knight gone cold in love;
It was an iceberg with long arms unseen,
That felt the deep for vessels far away.
All things seemed strange, I stared like any child
That pores on some old face and sees a world
Which its familiar granddad and his dame
Hid with their love and laughter until then.
My feet had not yet felt the cruel rocks
Beneath the pleasant moss I seemed to tread.
But soon my ears grew weary of that din,
My eyes grew tired of all that flesh and stone;
And, as a snail that crawls on a smooth stalk,
Will reach the end and find a sharpened thorn—
So did I reach the cruel end at last.
I saw the starving mother and her child,
Who feared that Death would surely end its sleep,
And cursed the wolf of Hunger with her moans.
And yet, methought, when first I entered there,
Into that city with my wondering mind,
How marvellous its many sights and sounds;
The traffic with its sound of heavy seas
That have and would again unseat the rocks.
How common then seemed Nature's hills and fields
Compared with these high domes and even streets,
And churches with white towers and bodies black.
The traffic's sound was music to my ears;
A sound of where the white waves, hour by hour,
Attack a reef of coral rising yet;
Or where a mighty warship in a fog,
Steams into a large fleet of little boats.
Aye, and that fog was strange and wonderful,
That made men blind and grope their way at noon.
I saw that City with fierce human surge,
With millions of dark waves that still spread out
To swallow more of their green boundaries.
Then came a day that noise so stirred my soul,
I called them hellish sounds, and thought red war
Was better far than peace in such a town.

To hear that din all day, sometimes my mind
Went crazed, and it seemed strange, as I were lost
In some vast forest full of chattering apes.
How sick I grew to hear that lasting noise,
And all those people forced across my sight,

Knowing the acres of green fields and woods
That in some country parts outnumbered men;
In half an hour ten thousand men I passed—
More than nine thousand should have been green trees.
There on a summer's day I saw such crowds
That where there was no man man's shadow was;
Millions all cramped together in one hive,
Storing, methought, more bitter stuff than sweet.
The air was foul and stale; from their green homes
Young blood had brought its fresh and rosy cheeks,
Which soon turned colour, like blue streams in flood.
Aye, solitude, black solitude indeed,
To meet a million souls and know not one;
This world must soon grow stale to one compelled
To look all day at faces strange and cold.
Oft full of smoke that town; its summer's day
Was darker than a summer's night at sea;
Poison was there, and still men rushed for it,
Like cows for acorns that have made them sick.
That town was rich and old; man's flesh was cheap,
But common earth was dear to buy one foot.
If I must be fenced in, then let my fence
Be some green hedgerow; under its green sprays,
That shake suspended, let me walk in joy—
As I do now, in these dear months I love.

W.H. Davies – A Short Biography

William Henry Davies, but always known as W. H. Davies, was born at 6, Portland Street in the Pillgwenlly district of Newport, Monmouthshire, Wales, a busy port on July 3rd, 1871.

In November 1874, when he was three, his father, an iron moulder, died. The following year his mother, Mary Anne Davies, remarried to become Mrs Joseph Hill. She agreed that the three children should pass into the care of the paternal grandparents, Francis and Lydia Davies, who ran the nearby Church House Inn at 14, Portland Street.

Davies seemed to find childhood difficult. By the age of 13 he was arrested, part of a gang of five schoolmates, and charged with stealing handbags. He was given twelve strokes of the birch. The following year, 1885, Davies wrote his first poem; "Death".

However, he did have an appetite for reading and as he later recounted, at the age of 14, when left to sit with his dying grandfather that he missed the moment of his grandfather's passing as he was too engrossed in reading "a very interesting book of wild adventure".

In November 1886 with his schooling finished he began a five-year apprenticeship to a local picture-frame maker. He never settled at this craft or indeed any regular work. His yearning was to travel.

Davies was apparently a difficult and somewhat delinquent young man, and made many requests to his grandmother to lend him funds so that he could sail to America. Eventually in 1893 through his own resources he reached America. In a half dozen years, he crossed the Atlantic at least annually by working on cattle ships. He travelled through many of the states, sometimes begging, sometimes taking seasonal work, but would often spend any savings on a drinking spree with a fellow traveller.

His turning point arrived when, after a week of rambling in London, he came across a newspaper story about the riches to be made in the Klondike and immediately set off to make his fortune in Canada. Attempting to jump a freight train at Renfrew, Ontario, on March 20th, 1899, with fellow tramp Three-fingered Jack, he lost his footing and his right foot was crushed under the wheels of the train. The leg later had to be amputated below the knee and he wore a wooden prosthetic leg thereafter.

Davies later wrote: "I bore this accident with an outward fortitude that was far from the true state of my feelings. Thinking of my present helplessness caused me many a bitter moment, but I managed to impress all comers with a false indifference ... I was soon home again, having been away less than four months; but all the wildness had been taken out of me, and my adventures after this were not of my own seeking, but the result of circumstances."

He returned to Britain, living a rough life in London shelters and doss-houses. Unsure of the possible reaction from his fellow tramps to his poetry, he would often feign sleep as he mentally composed his poems for later commitment to paper. At one stage he borrowed money to have his poems printed on loose sheets of paper, which he then tried to sell door-to-door through the streets of residential London. The enterprise failed.

Davies published his first book of poetry, The Soul's Destroyer, in 1905, again by means of his own savings. By cutting back expenditure to almost nothing and living the life of a tramp for six months (with the first draft of the book hidden in his pocket), and a small loan of funds from his inheritance it was eventually published. The volume was largely ignored and he took to posting copies to prospective wealthy customers taken from the pages of Who's Who, and asking them to send a half crown, in return. He eventually managed to sell 60 of the 200 copies printed.

One of the copies was sent to Arthur Adcock, a journalist with the Daily Mail. Adcock later wrote in his essay "Gods of Modern Grub Street", that he "recognised that there were crudities and even doggerel in it, there was also in it some of the freshest and most magical poetry to be found in modern books". He sent the half crown and asked Davies to meet him. Adcock is still regarded as "the man who discovered Davies". The first trade edition of The Soul's Destroyer was published in 1907. Further editions followed in 1908 and 1910.

On October 12th, 1905 Davies met the poet Edward Thomas, then literary critic for the Daily Chronicle. Thomas rented for Davies the tiny two-roomed "Stidulph's Cottage", in Egg Pie Lane, in the second week of February 1907. The cottage was "only two meadows off" from Thomas' own house. Thomas adopted the role of protective guardian for Davies, on one occasion even arranging for the manufacture, by a local wheelwright, of a replacement wooden leg. Thomas also made every effort to promote Davis's talent into a meaningful career.

In 1907, the manuscript of The Autobiography of a Super-Tramp drew the attention of George Bernard Shaw, who agreed to write a preface. It was because of Shaw that Davies' contract with the publishers was rewritten to allow the author to retain the serial rights, reversion of all rights after three years, royalties of fifteen per cent of selling price and a non-returnable advance of twenty-five pounds. He was also to have a say on the style of illustrations, advertisement layouts and cover designs. The original publisher, Duckworth and Sons, refused these demands and the book was released instead by Fifield.

In 1911, Davies was awarded a Civil List Pension of £50, which later increased to £100 and then to £150.

In London Davies started to spend more time in literary circles, even starting an autograph collection. The influential Georgian poetry publisher, Edward Marsh, introduced Davies to DH Lawrence and his wife Frieda in July, 1913 and Davies was able to secure an autograph from DH Lawrence

Lawrence was captivated by Davies and later invited him to join them in Germany. Despite this early enthusiasm Lawrence's opinion waned after reading Foliage and further after reading Nature Poems he noted that the verses seemed "so thin, one can hardly feel them".

After several temporary abodes, Davies, in early 1914, rented rooms at 14 Great Russell Street, previously the residence of Charles Dickens in London's Bloomsbury district. Here in a two-room apartment, infested with mice and rats, and next door to a noisy Belgian prostitute, he lived from early 1916 until 1921. Davies now expanded his career by giving a series of public readings of his work, alongside others such as Hilaire Belloc and W. B. Yeats and also impressed his fellow poet Ezra Pound.

Davies was always a person of some fascination by fellow artists. His head was cast in bronze in 1916 by the famed sculptor Jacob Epstein's works.

He enjoyed the company of literary men and their conversation, particularly in the rarefied atmosphere of the Café Royal. Another haunt was the Mont Blanc in Soho and with it the company of W. H. Hudson, Edward Garrett and others.

In the last months of 1921, Davies moved to Brook Street to rent rooms from the Quaker poet Olaf Baker. He began to find prolonged work difficult, however, suffering from increased bouts of rheumatism and other ailments.

On February 5th, 1923, he married 23-year-old Helen Matilda Payne, at the Registry Office in East Grinstead in Sussex. His book Young Emma chronicles the relationship in a very frank and revealing way. Having second thoughts he retrieved the book from the publishers and it was only published after Helens death several decades later. He had met her near Marble Arch decanting from a bus wearing a "saucy-looking little velvet cap with tassels". At the time Helen was unmarried and pregnant. Whilst living with Davies in London, before the couple were married, Helen suffered an almost fatal miscarriage.

The couple lived quietly and happily, moving first to Sevenoaks, then to "Malpas House", Oxted in Surrey and finally moving through a series of five different residences at Nailsworth in Gloucestershire. The couple had no children.

Davies was always keen to find different modes to express his work. He made over a dozen broadcasts for the BBC, reading his own work, between 1924 and 1940.

In 1925, a further volume of auto-biography, Later Days, describes the beginnings of Davies' career as a writer and his acquaintance with Hilaire Belloc, George Bernard Shaw and Walter de la Mare, amongst many others.

By now his reputation had also made him "the most painted literary man of his day", drawn and painted by many including Augustus John.

In 1930 he edited the poetry anthology Jewels of Song for Cape, choosing works by more than 120 different poets, and including William Blake, Thomas Campion, William Shakespeare, Alfred, Lord Tennyson and W. B. Yeats. Of his own poems he selected only "The Kingfisher" and "Leisure".

Davies returned to Newport, in September 1938, for the unveiling of a plaque in his honour at the Church House Inn. An address was given by the Poet Laureate John Masefield. He was still unwell, however, and this proved to be his last public appearance.

About three months before he died, Davies was visited at Glendower by Gordon Woodhouse and the Sitwells, Davies being too ill to travel to dinner at Nether Lypiatt. Osbert Sitwell noted that Davies looked "very ill" but that ".... his head, so typical of him in its rustic and nautical boldness, with the black hair now greying a little, but as stiff as ever, surrounding his high bony forehead, seemed to have acquired an even more sculptural quality." Helen privately explained to Sitwell that Davies' heart showed "alarming symptoms of weakness" caused, according to his doctors, by the dragging weight of his wooden leg. Helen had been careful to keep the true extent of the medical diagnosis from her husband.

Davies himself confided in Sitwell: "I've never been ill before, really, except when I had that accident and lost my leg ... And, d'you know, I grow so irritable when I've got that pain, I can't bear the sound of people's voices. ... Sometimes I feel I should like to turn over on my side and die."

W. H. Davies' health continued to deteriorate and he died, on September 26th, 1940, at the age of 69.

W. H. Davies – A Concise Bibliography

The Soul's Destroyer and Other Poems (of the author, The Farmhouse, 1905) (also Alston Rivers, 1907),
New Poems, 1907
Nature Poems, 1908
The Autobiography of a Super-Tramp, 1908
How It Feels To Be Out of Work (The English Review, 1 Dec 1908)
Beggars, 1909
Farewell to Poesy, 1910
Songs of Joy and Others, 1911
A Weak Woman, 1911
The True Traveller, 1912
Foliage: Various Poems,
Nature, 1914
The Bird of Paradise,
Child Lovers,

Collected Poems,
A Poet's Pilgrimage (or A Pilgrimage In Wales), 1918
Forty New Poems, 1918
Raptures, 1918
The Song of Life, 1920
The Captive Lion and Other Poems, 1921
Form (Editor Davies and Austin O Spare), Vol 1, Numbers 1, 2 & 3, 1921/1922
The Hour of Magic, 1922
Shorter Lyrics of the Twentieth Century, 1900–1922. Editor Davies, 1922
True Travellers. A Tramp's Opera in Three Acts, 1923
Collected Poems, 1st Series, 1923
Collected Poems, 2nd Series, 1923
Selected Poems, 1923
'Poets and Critics' - New Statesman, 21, Sept 8th 1923
What I Gained and Lost By Not Staying At School. Teachers World 29, June 1923
Secrets, 1924
Moll Flanders. Introduction by Davies, 1924
A Poet's Alphabet, 1925
Later Days, 1925
Augustan Book of Poetry: Thirty Selected Poems,
The Song of Love, 1926
The Adventures of Johnny Walker, 1926
A Poet's Calendar, 1927
Dancing Mad, 1927
The Collected Poems of W. H. Davies, 1928
Moss and Feather, 1928
Forty Nine Poems, 1928
Selected Poems, Arranged by Edward Garnett, introduction by Davies, 1928
Ambition and Other Poems, 1929
Jewels of Song (Editor. Anthology, 1930
In Winter, 1931
Poems 1930–31, 1931
The Lover's Song Book, 1933
My Birds, 1933
My Garden, 1933
'Memories' - School, 1, Nov 1933
The Poems of W. H. Davies: A Complete Collection, 1934
Love Poems, 1935
The Birth of Song, 1936
'Epilogue' to The Romance of the Echoing Wood, 1937
An Anthology of Short Poems (Editor. Anthology, 1938
The Loneliest Mountain, 1939
The Poems of W. H. Davies, 1940
Common Joys and Other Poems, 1941
Collected Poems of W. H. Davies, 1943